Fun Fan Facts:
The Unofficial NBA Edition

Phoenix Suns

Everything Young Suns Fans Should Know

By: Jake Liam

Dedication

For every fan who has watched three Finals and still shows up in orange and purple believing this is finally the year. The desert does not quit. Neither do you.

THE NBA BY THE NUMBERS

MOST NBA CHAMPIONSHIPS*

CELTICS (18) †

LAKERS (17)

WARRIORS (7)

BULLS (6)

SPURS (5)

As of the 2024-25 Season. † One Trophy = 4 Championships.

NBA HISTORY SNAPSHOT

1946 — NBA Founded

1954 — Shot Clock Introduced

1979 — 3-Point Line Added

2023 — NBA Cup Introduced

BIG NUMBERS

$156 million
Stephen Curry's est. earnings in the 24-25 season

7'7"
Tallest player in NBA history (Gheorghe Mureşan & Manute Bol)

30 | 4 | 82

30 — Teams Competing in the NBA

4 — Playoff Rounds

82 — Games Per Season

PHOENIX SUNS

IN THE NBA

- FOUNDED: 1968 †
- NBA TITLES: 0
- CONFERENCE TITLES: 3*

36 Playoff Appearances

*† Founding dates are complicated & may cause arguments at Thanksgiving. Ask someone born before color TV. All Titles reflect pre-relocation franchise history. * As of 2024-25 Season.*

NBA ALL-TIME MVP LEADERS

KAREEM ABDUL-JABBAR (6) ★ MICHAEL JORDAN (5) ★ BILL RUSSELL (5)

EASTERN CONFERENCE

Atlantic – **Celtics**
Atlantic – **Nets**
Atlantic – **Knicks**
Atlantic – **76ers**
Atlantic – **Raptors**
Central – **Bulls**
Central – **Cavaliers**
Central – **Pistons**
Central – **Pacers**
Central – **Bucks**
Southeast – **Hawks**
Southeast – **Hornets**
Southeast – **Heat**
Southeast – **Magic**
Southeast – **Wizards**

WESTERN CONFERENCE

Pacific – **Lakers**
Pacific – **Clippers**
Pacific – **Warriors**
Pacific – **Suns**
Pacific – **Kings**
Northwest – **Nuggets**
Northwest – **Timberwolves**
Northwest – **Thunder**
Northwest – **Trail Blazers**
Northwest – **Jazz**
Southwest – **Mavericks**
Southwest – **Rockets**
Southwest – **Spurs**
Southwest – **Pelicans**
Southwest – **Grizzlies**

Introduction

Welcome, fans! Whether you're new to cheering for the Phoenix Suns or you've been bleeding purple and orange your whole life, this book is packed with fun, exciting, and surprising facts about your favorite team. Get ready to impress your friends and family with everything you know about the Suns.

Quick Timeout

This book is packed with stats. Like, A LOT of stats. Every fact was checked, double-checked, and triple-checked. But here's the thing about basketball history: not everyone agrees on everything. Ask someone who watched games before color TV and someone who grew up with instant replay and you'll get two completely different answers. My dad, stepdad, uncle, and grandpa all argued about the same fact. Four people. Four answers. All of them think they're right. So if you spot something that doesn't match what you've heard, congratulations. You might be a bigger fan than the people who helped make this book. And honestly? That's pretty cool.

HOW IT WORKS

THE SEASON

82 Games. One Goal.

Each team plays 82 games.
Win enough to make the
Playoffs.
Every game counts!

PLAYOFFS

30 Teams. 16 Make It.

8 per conference make the playoffs.
Win=Advance | Lose=Go Home
Best record
gets home court!

PLAYOFF ROUNDS

Best of 7. Win 4 or Go Home.

4 rounds of pure pressure.
Every series is do-or-die!

OVERTIME?

5 More Minutes.

Keep playing until
someone pulls ahead.
No ties. Ever.

THE FINALS

One Series. One Champion.

Winner lifts the Trophy.
Legend status unlocked.

How the NBA Works

At first glance, basketball feels simple. Ten players. One ball. Two hoops. Go.

Then the NBA adds the layers.

An 82-game regular season. A draft where bad teams pick first. Playoffs that last two full months. Superstars who can change everything with one trade. Dynasties that rise, fall, and rise again.

And somehow, it all works.

The NBA is built on one big idea: every team gets a chance to reset, reload, and rise again. No relegation. No dropping down to a lower league. Just basketball, every night, from October through June.

It is a league designed for drama, stars, and comebacks. And once you understand the flow, it is impossible to stop watching.

The League Setup

The NBA has 30 teams, spread across the United States and Canada. Those teams are split into two conferences:

- Eastern Conference
- Western Conference

Each conference has three divisions, mostly based on geography. Divisions matter for scheduling, but not as much as they used to.

Every team plays 82 regular season games, usually from October through April. Home games. Road games. Back-to-back nights. Long road trips. The season is a marathon before the sprint even starts.

Win games, and you climb the standings. Lose too many, and the pressure builds fast.

How Games Are Played

An NBA game has four quarters, each lasting 12 minutes. That means 48 minutes of game time, plus timeouts, free throws, and the occasional coach argument that adds another 20 minutes nobody planned for.

Scoring is simple:

- A shot inside the three-point line is worth 2 points
- A shot beyond the arc is worth 3 points
- Free throws are worth 1 point

If the score is tied at the end of regulation, the game goes to overtime, which lasts 5 minutes. Still tied? Another overtime. Keep going until someone wins.

There is a shot clock too. Teams have 24 seconds to take a shot. No standing around. No holding the ball forever. Keep it moving.

The Regular Season Race

The regular season is long for a reason. It tests everything.

Depth. Health. Focus. Patience.

Teams play opponents from both conferences, but they face conference rivals more often. By the end of the season, each conference's top teams have earned their playoff spots the hard way.

The goal is simple: make the playoffs. But there is a twist.

The NBA Cup

In 2023, the NBA added something new to the middle of the season. Something with actual stakes. They called it the In-Season Tournament, now known as the NBA Cup.

It works like this: Every team plays a small group stage during November and December, with special court designs that look like nothing else in basketball. The best teams advance to a knockout round held in Las Vegas.

The winners split a prize pool. Players earn bonus money. And for the first time, a team could lift a trophy before the playoffs even started.

Some fans are still warming up to it. Some players love it. But the moment a team starts treating it seriously and a crowd shows up buzzing in December, it feels like something.

Which, honestly, sounds about right.

The Play-In Tournament

Instead of sending the top eight teams from each conference straight to the playoffs, the NBA added something new. The Play-In Tournament.

Here is how it works:

- Teams ranked 1 through 6 in each conference are safe
- Teams ranked 7 through 10 fight for the final two playoff spots

The 7 and 8 seeds have an advantage. Win once and you are in. Lose and you still get one more shot. The 9 and 10 seeds have to win twice in a row just to earn a first-round matchup.

It turns the end of the season into a sprint. Every game suddenly matters more. Fans love it. Coaches age rapidly.

The NBA Playoffs

Once the playoffs begin, everything tightens.

Sixteen teams enter. Eight from each conference. Every round is a best-of-seven games series. That means the first team to win four games moves on:

- First Round
- Conference Semifinals
- Conference Finals
- NBA Finals

Home-court advantage matters. Crowds get louder. Rotations get shorter. Superstars play heavier minutes. One bad quarter can flip a series. One great performance can define a career.

By the time the NBA Finals arrive in June, only two teams are left. One from the East. One from the West.

Four wins away from a championship. Four wins away from history.

The NBA Draft: Hope Begins Here

Here is where the NBA gets clever. Every summer, new players enter the league through the NBA Draft. Teams take turns selecting college players, international stars, and teenagers straight out of high school.

The teams that finished with the worst records get the best odds to pick early through the Draft Lottery. It is not guaranteed, but it gives struggling franchises a real shot at changing their future with one pick.

That means one bad season does not doom you forever. It might actually change everything. Some franchises are rebuilt by a single draft night moment.

Hope shows up wearing a new jersey.

No Relegation. All Pressure.

Unlike many global sports leagues, NBA teams never drop down to a lower league. They always stay in the NBA.

That does not mean there is no pressure.

Fans remember losing seasons. Owners make changes. Coaches get replaced. Players get traded. Every year is a test of direction, patience, and belief.

Stars, Systems, and Showtime

The NBA is famous for its stars. But stars do not win alone.

Teams need chemistry. Coaches need systems. Role players need to deliver on the biggest stages. One injury. One hot streak. One trade deadline deal. Any of it can flip a season.

That balance between individual brilliance and team basketball is what makes the league special.

Fast breaks. Buzzer-beaters. Game 7s. And moments that get replayed forever. That is the NBA.

Once you get the flow, it is pure electricity.

Phoenix Suns Facts

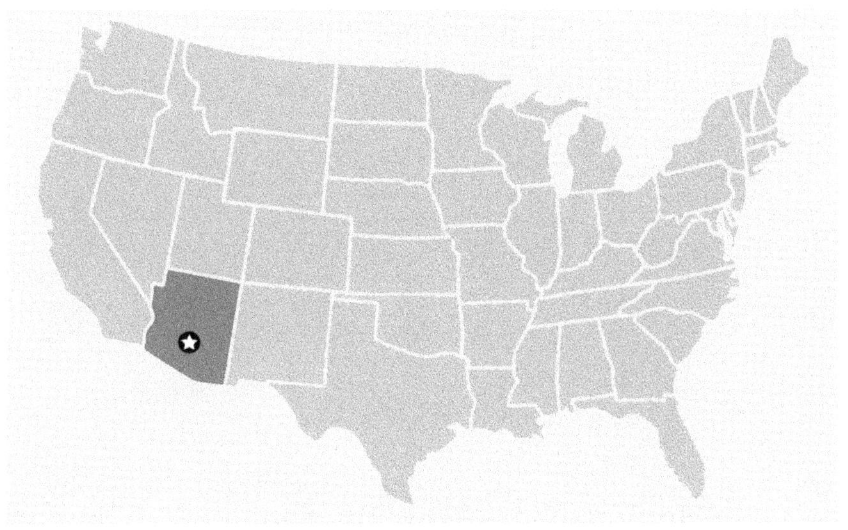

Home City

Phoenix, Arizona

Home City Metro Area Population

about 5 million

Home Arena

Footprint Center

Max Capacity: 17,071

Famous Local Food

Sonoran hot dogs, green chile, Navajo tacos, chimichangas

Conference / Division

Western / Pacific

Chapter 1: Desert Born

1. The Coin Flip That Changed Everything

In 1968, the NBA awarded expansion franchises to two new teams: the Phoenix Suns and the Milwaukee Bucks. Both teams were brand new, both were starting from scratch, and both had exactly zero players worth mentioning yet. To decide which team got the first overall pick in the 1969 draft, the league did what any billion-dollar sports organization would do when facing a major decision: they flipped a coin.

The prize was Lew Alcindor, a seven-foot-two college center out of UCLA who would later change his name to Kareem Abdul-Jabbar and go on to become the NBA's all-time leading scorer. Phoenix called heads. The coin landed tails. Milwaukee got Kareem. Phoenix got the second pick and selected Neal Walk, who had a perfectly respectable career that absolutely nobody has a poster of on their bedroom wall.

Here is the part that stings just a little extra: the Suns actually requested to lose the flip, believing that finishing last in the regular season would give them a better draft position the following year. The basketball gods heard that logic and filed it directly in the trash. Phoenix lost the flip, lost the pick, and spent the next several decades wondering what might have been if that coin had just gone the other way.

2. The Young Team That Shocked Everyone

Eight years into their existence, the Phoenix Suns did something that nobody, including probably the Phoenix Suns, fully expected. They made the NBA Finals.

The 1976 Suns were not supposed to be there. They had finished the regular season as a middle-of-the-pack team, snuck through the playoffs, and found themselves facing the Boston Celtics for the championship. Boston had won more titles than any franchise in NBA history. Phoenix had won exactly zero. On paper it was not a fair fight.

What happened next produced one of the most celebrated games in Finals history. Game 5 went to triple overtime in a contest so chaotic, so back-and-forth, and so completely unhinged that a fan ran onto the court during the madness and punched a referee, which somehow was not even the most talked-about moment of the night. The Suns lost the series in six games but announced to the entire league

that something was being built in the Arizona desert.
The full story of that game deserves its own chapter,
and it gets one later in this book.

3. From Coliseum to Footprint

The Suns have played in three different arenas across
their history, which is not unusual for a franchise that
has been around since 1968, but the journey between
buildings tracks almost perfectly with the team's rise in
the city's consciousness.

They started at Veterans Memorial Coliseum, a building
that opened in 1965 and was originally designed more
with livestock shows and state fairs in mind than
professional basketball. It held about 14,000 fans and
did the job for nearly two decades. In 1992, the Suns
moved into a brand new downtown arena that went
through several corporate name changes over the
years, from America West Arena to US Airways Center
to Talking Stick Resort Arena, before finally landing on
Footprint Center in 2021.

Footprint Center holds around 18,000 fans for
basketball and sits in the heart of downtown Phoenix,
part of a sports and entertainment district that has
grown significantly around it. The building was

renovated ahead of the 2021-22 season with significant upgrades to fan areas and the court-level experience. For a franchise that spent its first decade playing in a converted fairground, arriving at a modern downtown arena was its own kind of statement about how seriously Phoenix had come to take its basketball team.

4. The Colors That Own a Desert

Purple and orange should not work together. In most design conversations, putting those two colors next to each other would get someone gently redirected toward something more sensible. The Phoenix Suns ignored that conversation entirely and produced one of the most recognizable color combinations in professional sports.

The original uniform set debuted in 1968 with a purple and orange palette that leaned heavily into the Arizona sunset aesthetic, which is one of the few places on earth where those colors appear naturally and look completely correct. The team has updated and tweaked the look several times over the decades, cycling through different shades and alternate uniforms, including a black-heavy set in the 1990s that was very much a product of its era.

The current identity leans into the classic orange and purple combination with modern updates, and the throwback versions of the old uniforms remain some of the most popular alternate jerseys in the league when they surface. Few teams can say their original color scheme from 1968 is still the most beloved version more than fifty years later. The Suns can.

Phoenix Suns fans turn the arena into a sea of orange. Shirts. Hats. Towels. Everywhere you look, it's orange. In fact, fans call it "Planet Orange." If you're reading this book in black and white, trust us on this one. The crowd is very orange. *Photo: Phoenix Suns fans during the 2010 NBA Playoffs. Photograph via Wikimedia Commons. Licensed under CC BY-SA 2.0. Source: Wikimedia Commons.*

5. A Desert That Learned to Love Basketball

Phoenix is not an obvious basketball city. It is a sprawling, sun-baked metropolis in the middle of the Sonoran Desert, where the summers are so hot that asphalt can soften and outdoor activities are something people discuss in the past tense from June through September. The idea that this city would become a passionate NBA market required a specific set of ingredients to come together over several decades.

The Suns arrived in 1968 as one of the few major professional sports franchises in the state. Arizona did not have an NFL team until 1988. There was no MLB team until 1998. For a long time, the Suns were the biggest game in town, which meant that when they were good, the whole city paid attention. The Charles Barkley era in the early 1990s, which brought a genuine championship contender to Phoenix for the first time, accelerated that relationship significantly.

By the time the Steve Nash era arrived in the mid-2000s with one of the most entertaining offenses the league had ever seen, Phoenix was a legitimate basketball city with a fanbase that had lived through enough near-misses to make the good times feel genuinely earned. The desert learned basketball slowly, then all at once.

6. Charles Barkley: The Round Mound of Rebound (1992-1996)

Charles Barkley was listed at six feet six inches, which is a perfectly respectable height for a human being but makes very little sense for someone who dominated NBA power forwards for over a decade. He weighed somewhere in the neighborhood of 250 to 260 pounds depending on the season and had a physical style that made opposing big men feel like they had walked into a disagreement they had not fully prepared for.

Barkley arrived in Phoenix via trade from Philadelphia in 1992 and immediately turned the Suns into a championship contender. In the 1992-93 season he won the NBA's Most Valuable Player award, leading Phoenix to a franchise-record 62 wins and all the way to the Finals against the Chicago Bulls and Michael Jordan. The series went six games, and the Suns came closer than the final result suggests. More on that in Chapter 3.

What made Barkley something beyond a great player was the personality that came with the basketball. He was funny, opinionated, and constitutionally incapable of giving a boring answer to any question. He became one of the most quoted figures in the sport and one of the most beloved athletes in Phoenix history despite only spending four seasons there. He was inducted into the Naismith Basketball Hall of Fame in 2006. The city of Phoenix never entirely stopped being glad that trade happened.

7. Steve Nash: The Point Guard Who Rewrote the Rules (1996-1998, 2004-2012)

Steve Nash grew up in Victoria, British Columbia, which is a beautiful part of Canada and not historically known as a launching pad for two-time NBA Most Valuable Players. Nash became one anyway, which should tell you something about what happens when exceptional talent meets exceptional work ethic in a person who clearly did not receive the memo about what was supposed to be possible.

Nash was drafted by Phoenix in 1996, spent two seasons learning the league, then was traded to Dallas where he developed into one of the best point guards in the game. The Suns brought him back in 2004 as a free agent and handed him the keys to an offense designed by coach Mike D'Antoni that would change how NBA teams thought about pace, spacing, and the three-point shot. Nash won back-to-back MVP awards in 2005 and 2006, making him one of a small group of players in league history to win the award in consecutive seasons.

He was not the fastest player on the court. He was not the most athletic. He was listed at six feet one inch, which in NBA terms is closer to the catering staff than the starting lineup. What Nash had was a feel for the game so precise that teammates who played with him regularly described it as something they had never quite experienced before or since. He made everyone around him look better, which is the most underrated skill in basketball and one of the hardest to measure.

8. Devin Booker: The Kid Who Stayed (2015-present)

Most NBA stars reach a point where a bigger market, a better team, or a larger contract somewhere else starts to look appealing. Devin Booker reached that point more than once and chose Phoenix every time, which in the modern NBA is not a small thing.

Booker was drafted 13th overall in 2015 out of Kentucky, arriving in Phoenix as a teenager on a team that was nowhere near playoff contention. He spent several years developing his game while the franchise rebuilt around him, and by the time the Suns became relevant again in the early 2020s, he had grown into one of the most complete scoring guards in the league. He made his first All-Star team in 2020 and led Phoenix to the NBA Finals in 2021 as the unquestioned leader of the roster.

What separates Booker from other high-level scorers is the range of ways he can hurt a defense. Mid-range jumpers, pull-up threes, floaters in traffic, trips to the free throw line. He does not rely on one signature move that opposing coaches can scheme against. He scored 70 points in a single game before he turned 21, a story that deserves its own full telling and gets one in Chapter 3. He has been the face of the franchise for the better part of a decade, which is exactly what the organization hoped for when they drafted a teenager from Kentucky and asked him to be patient.

9. Kevin Johnson: The Heartbeat of a Generation (1988-2000)

Before Charles Barkley arrived and before Steve Nash changed everything, the player who defined Phoenix basketball for a full generation of fans was Kevin Johnson, a point guard from Sacramento, California who gave the Suns twelve seasons of electric, fearless basketball.

Johnson arrived via trade from Cleveland in 1988 in a deal that sent fan favorite Larry Nance to the Cavaliers. The reaction from Phoenix fans was not immediately warm. Then Johnson started playing, and the reaction changed. He was quick in a way that made highlight reels look slow, a blur in the open court and an absolute menace in pick-and-roll situations that opposing defenses never fully solved.

He made three All-Star teams as a Sun and was consistently among the best point guards in the Western Conference throughout his peak years. Johnson played through injuries that would have shortened other careers and delivered some of the most memorable playoff performances in franchise history. He later became the mayor of Sacramento, which is either a remarkable second act or proof that some people simply refuse to stop being impressive once they start.

10. Amar'e Stoudemire: The Man Who Made Seven Seconds Terrifying (2002-2010)

The Seven Seconds or Less offense that Steve Nash ran in the mid-2000s required one specific ingredient beyond pace and shooting: a big man fast enough and skilled enough to make the whole thing work in the paint. Amar'e Stoudemire was that ingredient, and without him, the most famous offense in modern Suns history does not function the way it did.

Stoudemire was drafted ninth overall in 2002 directly out of high school, skipping college entirely, which was still permitted at the time and which the Suns did not regret for a single minute. He was a physical force around the basket, an above-the-rim finisher who could catch Nash's passes in traffic at full speed and finish before the defense had time to react. In the 2004-05 season he won the NBA's Most Improved Player award. The following season, with Nash running the point, the Suns became the most entertaining team in the league.

Stoudemire dealt with significant knee injuries during his Phoenix tenure that limited what should have been some of his best seasons, and the Suns' inability to win a championship during that window remains one of the more painful near-misses in franchise history. He left for the New York Knicks in 2010. The offense that he and Nash ran together, for the seasons it was fully healthy and operational, was something opposing coaches genuinely dreaded preparing for on short rest.

11. The Series That Still Hurts

The 1993 NBA Finals matched the Phoenix Suns against the Chicago Bulls, which meant they were matched against Michael Jordan at the absolute peak of his powers, which, in hindsight, was not the ideal scheduling situation for anyone hoping to win a championship.

Phoenix had the best record in the league that year and Charles Barkley had just won MVP. The Suns won Games 1 and 2 in Chicago, which almost never happened to Jordan-era Bulls teams, and the series stayed tight all the way to Game 6. With Phoenix needing a win to force Game 7, the Suns had the ball and a chance in the final seconds. John Paxson caught a pass on the wing with 3.9 seconds left and hit a three-pointer that gave Chicago the title. The Suns lost by three points. One shot. Three points.

Barkley finished the series having given everything a player can give in six games and walked away without a ring. He never made it back to the Finals. The 1993 Suns remain one of the most talented teams in franchise history, and that Paxson shot remains one of the more quietly devastating moments in Phoenix sports memory. Close is only a good outcome in horseshoes, and the Suns were not playing horseshoes.

12. The Greatest Game Nobody Under 50 Saw Live

Game 5 of the 1976 NBA Finals between the Phoenix Suns and Boston Celtics is regularly listed among the greatest games ever played, which is remarkable for a game that most current NBA fans have never watched a single second of.

The Suns trailed Boston three games to one heading into Game 5 and needed a win to stay alive. What followed was 63 minutes of basketball that went through regulation, then overtime, then a second overtime, then a third. Triple overtime. In a Finals elimination game. The lead changed hands repeatedly and the Celtics eventually won 128-126, ending Phoenix's championship run. What made the game legendary was not just the length but the chaos packed inside it: a fan ran onto the court and punched a referee in the second overtime. The Suns were mistakenly called for a technical foul on a play where they had actually called timeout correctly, nearly costing them the game before the third period even started.

Phoenix lost the series and went home. But the 1976 Finals put the franchise on the national basketball map in a way that a quiet first-round exit never could have. Sometimes losing memorably is its own kind of achievement. The Suns would probably prefer a championship, but they will settle for being part of the most replayed Finals footage of the 1970s.

13. Seven Seconds or Less Changed Basketball

The specific number is the whole point. Seven seconds. That was the target time the Phoenix Suns under coach Mike D'Antoni allowed themselves to get a shot off after gaining possession. Not seven seconds as a rough guideline. Seven seconds as a philosophy, a religion, and a direct challenge to every defensive system in the NBA that relied on teams slowing down and thinking things through.

The 2004-05 and 2005-06 Suns averaged pace numbers that made the rest of the league look like they were playing in slow motion. The idea was simple and the execution was extraordinary: push the ball before the defense sets up, space the floor with shooters, and run pick-and-roll actions so fast that the opponent's rotations are always one step behind. It worked at a level that genuinely surprised people who thought they understood how NBA offenses functioned.

The ripple effects lasted for years after that specific roster broke up. Teams around the league began studying the Suns' approach and incorporating elements of it. The modern NBA, with its emphasis on pace, three-point volume, and ball movement, owes a significant debt to what D'Antoni and that group built in the desert. Phoenix never won the championship with that system, which is its own painful footnote. But the fingerprints of those Suns teams are visible on nearly every competitive NBA offense played today.

14. Seventy Points and a Loss

On March 24, 2017, Devin Booker scored 70 points in a single game. The Suns lost by three points.

That sentence alone is probably enough, but the details make it even more specifically absurd. Booker was 20 years old. The game was against the Boston Celtics. He scored his 60th point in the fourth quarter and kept going, reaching 70 with a late free throw in the final minute while the Suns were being outplayed in nearly every other aspect of the contest. He became the youngest player in NBA history to score 70 in a game and just the sixth player ever to reach that number at all, joining names like Wilt Chamberlain, David Thompson, and Elgin Baylor.

The loss, somehow, is part of what makes the story stick. A player drops 70 points, the kind of performance that stops conversations and breaks the internet, and the team still finds a way to lose the basketball game. It is the most Phoenix Suns outcome imaginable, delivered by the one player who would go on to carry the franchise out of exactly that kind of era. Booker finished the season on a team that won 24 games. He scored 70 in one of them, which is the basketball equivalent of running a five-minute mile and still missing the bus.

15. The Bubble Team That Almost Did It

The 2020-21 Phoenix Suns reached the NBA Finals in one of the more surprising deep runs of the decade, built on a roster that had been quietly assembled while most of the national conversation was focused elsewhere.

Chris Paul arrived in Phoenix via trade in the summer of 2020 at age 35, which is the age at which most point guards are making retirement plans. He proceeded to play some of the most efficient and composed basketball of his career, giving Booker something he had never quite had before: a co-pilot who had been through every kind of playoff situation imaginable and knew exactly how to navigate each one. The Suns won 51 regular season games and pushed through the first three rounds of the playoffs to reach the Finals for the first time since 1993.

They faced the Milwaukee Bucks, led by Giannis Antetokounmpo, and pushed the series to six games before Milwaukee closed it out. Giannis delivered one of the most dominant individual Finals performances in recent memory. Phoenix had their chances and could not quite convert them. The 2021 run remains the most recent time the Suns stood at the edge of the championship they have spent their entire existence chasing. The edge, unfortunately, is not the same as the top.

Chapter 4: Welcome to the Valley

16. The Gorilla Nobody Hired

In 1980, a man named Henry Rojas was working for a company that delivered singing telegrams. He was sent to Veterans Memorial Coliseum in Phoenix to deliver a telegram to someone in the building, showed up in a gorilla costume, and wandered onto the Suns' court during a game while looking for the recipient. The crowd laughed. The players laughed. Someone in the Suns organization made a phone call the next day.

The result is one of the most beloved mascot stories in professional sports. The gorilla, eventually named Go, became the official Suns mascot and spent decades performing elaborate dunks off trampolines, interacting with referees in ways that referees tolerated with varying degrees of patience, and becoming a fixture of Phoenix home games that fans of a certain generation consider inseparable from the Suns experience. He was inducted into the Mascot Hall of Fame, which is a real thing that exists.

The original performer, Bob Woolf, played the role for years before eventually passing the costume to successors. Most mascot performers are not publicly named during their tenure, so the lineage is not always fully documented. What is documented is that the whole thing started because a man in a gorilla suit got lost on his way to deliver a singing telegram. The NBA has seen stranger origin stories, but not many.

17. The Suspension That Changed a Playoff Series

On May 14, 2007, during Game 4 of the second-round playoff series between the Phoenix Suns and San Antonio Spurs, Robert Horry committed a hard foul on Steve Nash that sent Nash stumbling into the scorer's table. Amar'e Stoudemire and Boris Diaw both left the Phoenix bench area and stepped toward the court in reaction. They did not throw punches. They did not make contact with anyone. They took a few steps and were guided back.

Under NBA rules at the time, leaving the bench area during an altercation resulted in an automatic one-game suspension. Both Stoudemire and Diaw were suspended for Game 5. The Suns, who had been leading the series and were considered by many analysts to be the better team, lost Game 5 without two of their most important players and were eliminated from the playoffs.

The debate about whether the rule was applied fairly, whether the punishment fit the situation, and whether the outcome of that series would have been different with a full roster has never fully gone away in Phoenix. Horry received a two-game suspension, which meant he missed two games for the foul while Phoenix lost a rotation player for the game that ended their season. Whether the right call was made is a question with a different answer depending on who is wearing which team's jersey during the conversation.

18. The Valley Belongs to Everyone

Phoenix is one of the most diverse cities in the American Southwest, a metro area of roughly five million people drawn from across the country and across the world, and the Suns' fanbase reflects that in ways that the team has leaned into rather than ignored.

The rallying cry of Suns fans during the 2021 run was simply The Valley, referring to the Phoenix metropolitan area spread across the Sonoran Desert floor between mountain ranges. It showed up on alternate jerseys, on murals across the city, and in the social media language of a younger fanbase that connected with the Suns as something genuinely theirs. The Valley jerseys became some of the most popular alternates in the league almost immediately after they were introduced.

The fanbase sometimes calls itself the Valleyboyz, a loose collective identity for the loudest section of Phoenix supporters who bring an energy to home games that visiting teams occasionally mention in postgame press conferences. Not always positively. The Suns have built something in Phoenix that goes beyond wins and losses, a cultural identity tied to a city that has spent decades being underestimated by people who have never spent a week there. The desert has receipts.

19. Three Hundred Days of Sunshine and Solar Panels

Phoenix averages around 299 to 300 days of sunshine per year, which is either a blessing or a punishment depending on whether you enjoy the outdoors in July. It is also, as it turns out, an excellent argument for putting solar panels on a sports arena.

Footprint Center became one of the first major professional sports venues to install a significant solar energy system, with panels mounted on the arena roof and surrounding structures generating a portion of the building's power needs. For a franchise playing in a city that essentially receives free energy from the sky for ten months of the year, the decision made obvious sense. Whether it was driven primarily by environmental commitment or straightforward economics is a fair question, and the honest answer is probably both.

The solar initiative has been highlighted as part of a broader sustainability effort by the arena and its ownership, and Phoenix has continued to expand its renewable energy infrastructure since the initial installation. It is one of those franchise facts that does not show up in box scores or highlight reels but says something real about how the organization thinks about its footprint in a city that has enough actual footprint concerns just from the summer heat alone.

20. The Sonoran Hot Dog Deserves Its Own Trophy

Every great sports city has a food that belongs to it, the thing you eat at the game or near the game that you cannot quite replicate anywhere else. For Phoenix, that food is the Sonoran hot dog, and if you have never encountered one, the description sounds like a dare.

A Sonoran hot dog is a bacon-wrapped frankfurter, grilled until the bacon crisps up around the outside, nestled into a soft bolillo-style bun that is partially open at the top rather than split along the side. It is then topped with pinto beans, chopped tomatoes, onions, mayonnaise, mustard, and crumbled cotija cheese. It is a collaboration between Mexican and American food traditions that reflects exactly what the Phoenix metro area actually looks like demographically and culturally.

Street vendors and small stands around Phoenix have been serving them for decades, and the influence has spread to stadium concessions and restaurants throughout the city. Going to a Suns game in Phoenix and not eating a Sonoran hot dog is technically allowed but represents a significant missed opportunity. Charles Barkley, a man with famously strong opinions about food and most other things, has spoken positively about Phoenix's food scene during his time there. That is not a verified direct quote, but it would be surprising if he had not.

21. Devin Booker, Still Here, Still Standing

At some point during the messy middle years of the early 2020s, when the roster was changing and the coaches were cycling through and the championship window felt like it kept opening and closing without anyone actually climbing through it, Devin Booker signed a contract extension with Phoenix. He did not ask to be traded. He did not hint at greener pastures. He stayed.

Booker enters his eleventh season in a Suns uniform having already secured his place in franchise history. He averages over 25 points per game across his career, has made multiple All-Star teams, led Phoenix to the 2021 Finals, and scored 70 points in a single game before he turned 21. He has done all of this for one team, in one city, in a league where loyalty of that kind is genuinely rare.

His extension keeps him in Phoenix through the 2029-30 season, which means the franchise gets to build its next chapter around a player who has already survived enough organizational turbulence to know exactly what he signed up for. Some players need a championship to define a legacy. Booker is still writing his, and he is writing it in Phoenix whether the rest of the league expected that or not.

22. The New Owner and the Fresh Start

In early 2023, Mat Ishbia completed his purchase of the Phoenix Suns, taking over from longtime owner Robert Sarver in a deal that made Ishbia one of the newer faces in NBA ownership. He came from the mortgage industry, was a former walk-on basketball player at Michigan State under coach Tom Izzo, and arrived in Phoenix with an obvious enthusiasm for the product that he did not try to hide.

The years immediately following his arrival were complicated. The super team experiment involving Durant and Beal did not produce the results anyone hoped for, the team cycled through coaches, and the roster was significantly rebuilt heading into the 2025-26 season. New general manager Brian Gregory oversaw a dramatic roster reset, trading Durant to Houston in a seven-team deal that brought in young guard Jalen Green, defensive stopper Dillon Brooks, and seven-foot-two rookie Khaman Maluach among others.

First-year head coach Jordan Ott took over with a mandate to develop a younger core and rebuild the culture.

Whether that reset pays off is a question still being answered. What changed was the direction. Phoenix stopped trying to buy a championship overnight and started building something with a longer timeline. That is not always the most exciting announcement for a fanbase that has been waiting since 1968, but it is probably the more sustainable one.

23. The Super Team That Did Not Super

It made sense on paper. It really did. In 2023, the Phoenix Suns traded for Kevin Durant, one of the most gifted scorers in NBA history, to play alongside Devin Booker and Bradley Beal. Three All-Stars. One roster. Championship or bust.

The bust came faster than expected. The three players shared the floor together for only 23 games during the 2024-25 season due to injuries, lineup issues, and timing that never quite clicked. The team finished 36-46, missed the playoffs entirely, and fired coach Mike Budenholzer despite four years remaining on his contract, making him the second consecutive coach let go before his deal expired. Beal was eventually bought out and ended up with the LA Clippers. Durant was traded to Houston in a seven-team deal. The experiment lasted roughly two seasons and produced zero playoff wins.

The Super Team era is worth understanding not because it was a disaster but because it illustrates something real about how the NBA works. Star power alone does not win championships. Fit, timing, health, and a functional system all matter as much as individual talent. The Suns learned that the hard way, which is the most expensive way to learn anything in professional sports.

24. The New Core and What It Might Become

The roster that Phoenix assembled for the 2025-26 season looks almost nothing like the one that walked off the floor the year before, which was either terrifying or exciting depending on your appetite for change.

Jalen Green, acquired in the Durant trade, brings a scoring punch and youth to a backcourt alongside Booker. He averaged over 20 points per game in Houston and is still in his early twenties, which means the ceiling is genuinely unclear. Dillon Brooks arrived with a reputation as one of the more disruptive defensive players in the league and an edge that opposing teams do not enjoy dealing with on a nightly basis. Rookie Khaman Maluach, a seven-foot-two center from the NBA Africa Academy program who was selected tenth overall in the 2025 draft, represents a long-term project with an enormous physical foundation to build on.

The pieces are young, the roster is still finding its shape, and first-year coach Jordan Ott is doing the work of turning a collection of individuals into something with a shared identity. That process takes time. The Suns have gone through that process before and come out the other side with something worth watching. The pattern is familiar even if the faces are new.

25. The Ring That Is Still Missing

Three times in franchise history the Phoenix Suns have reached the NBA Finals. Three times they have come home without the trophy. The 1976 Celtics, the 1993 Bulls, the 2021 Bucks. Each one a different story. Each one the same ending.

No major professional sports franchise has a longer active championship drought in the NBA than the Suns, which is a complicated legacy for a team that has produced so much memorable basketball over five decades. The 1976 team was there before anyone expected them. The 1993 team was good enough to legitimately win. The 2021 team shocked the league and fell one round short of finishing it. All three came close. None of them finished it.

What the Suns have never done is stop believing that the ring is possible, which is either stubborn optimism or a very accurate read of their own potential depending on the season. The franchise has produced Hall of Famers, MVP winners, one of the most influential offensive systems in basketball history, and some of the most entertaining teams any era has seen. The only thing missing is the banner. In Phoenix, they have been waiting for it since 1968. The desert is patient. It has had to be.

Bonus Trivia Quiz!

You think you are a true Suns fan? Try this bonus quiz!

1. How did the Phoenix Suns decide which team got the first overall pick in the 1969 NBA Draft?

A) A play-in game between expansion teams
B) The team with the worst record from the previous season
C) A coin flip between Phoenix and Milwaukee
D) A blind draw at the NBA Draft Lottery

2. Who did the Suns select with the second overall pick in the 1969 draft after losing the coin flip?

A) Connie Hawkins
B) Neal Walk
C) Dick Van Arsdale
D) Paul Silas

3. What happened during Game 5 of the 1976 NBA Finals that made it one of the most chaotic games in league history?

A) The power went out for 20 minutes in the third quarter
B) A fan ran onto the court and punched a referee during overtime
C) Both head coaches were ejected in the fourth quarter
D) The game was suspended and finished the following day

4. Which arena did the Phoenix Suns play in during their first two decades before moving downtown?

A) Desert Sky Pavilion
B) Sun Devil Arena
C) Phoenix Municipal Stadium
D) Veterans Memorial Coliseum

5. What is the name of the Suns' mascot and how did he come to be?

A) Sunny, created by a fan design contest in 1980
B) Go, a gorilla who wandered onto the court while delivering a singing telegram
C) Cactus Jack, designed by the original ownership group in 1968
D) Flash, hired directly from a traveling circus in 1982

6. Charles Barkley won the NBA MVP award in which season with the Suns?

A) 1991-92
B) 1992-93
C) 1993-94
D) 1994-95

7. Steve Nash won back-to-back MVP awards in which two seasons?

A) 2003-04 and 2004-05
B) 2004-05 and 2005-06
C) 2005-06 and 2006-07
D) 2006-07 and 2007-08

8. What was the target time in seconds that defined Mike D'Antoni's famous Suns offense?

A) Five seconds
B) Six seconds
C) Seven seconds
D) Eight seconds

9. How old was Devin Booker when he scored 70 points in a single game?

A) 19
B) 20
C) 21
D) 22

10. The 2007 playoff suspension controversy involved which two Phoenix Suns players being suspended for leaving the bench area?

A) Steve Nash and Shawn Marion
B) Raja Bell and Kurt Thomas
C) Amar'e Stoudemire and Boris Diaw
D) Leandro Barbosa and Grant Hill

11. What is the name of the Suns' current home arena?

A) America West Arena
B) US Airways Center
C) Talking Stick Resort Arena
D) Footprint Center

12. Which team did Phoenix defeat in the 2021 NBA Playoffs to reach the Finals?

A) Los Angeles Lakers
B) Denver Nuggets
C) Los Angeles Clippers
D) Utah Jazz

13. What notable environmental feature does Footprint Center have that reflects Phoenix's geography?

A) A retractable roof that opens for outdoor games
B) Solar panels generating a portion of the arena's power
C) A built-in air conditioning system that uses underground water
D) Wind turbines along the exterior walls

14. Kevin Johnson, after retiring from basketball, went on to become what?

A) An NBA head coach
B) A television sports analyst
C) The mayor of Sacramento
D) A college athletic director

15. What was the outcome of the Suns' super team experiment with Durant, Booker, and Beal in 2024-25?

A) They won the Western Conference title before losing in the Finals
B) They reached the second round of the playoffs before being eliminated
C) They finished 36-46 and missed the playoffs entirely
D) They won 50 games but lost in the first round of the playoffs

Super Fan Secret Challenge

Only a true Suns fan will know this.

(No Answer Provided)

The 1976 Phoenix Suns made their unexpected Finals run largely on the strength of a core built through the draft. Their starting center that year was a homegrown Sun who spent his entire career in Phoenix, was drafted by the team in 1975, and later had his number retired by the franchise. He was not a superstar by national standards but was the backbone of every competitive Suns team through the late 1970s and 1980s. Who is this player, what number did he wear, and what college did he attend?

Answer Key

1. C) A coin flip between Phoenix and Milwaukee

2. B) Neal Walk

3. B) A fan ran onto the court and punched a referee during overtime

4. D) Veterans Memorial Coliseum

5. B) Go, a gorilla who wandered onto the court while delivering a singing telegram

6. B) 1992-93

7. B) 2004-05 and 2005-06

8. C) Seven seconds

9. B) 20

10. C) Amar'e Stoudemire and Boris Diaw

11. D) Footprint Center

12. C) Los Angeles Clippers

13. B) Solar panels generating a portion of the arena's power

14. C) The mayor of Sacramento

15. C) They finished 36-46 and missed the playoffs entirely

NBA PLAYOFF BRACKET

First Round	Semifinals	Conf. Finals	Finals	Conf. Finals	Semifinals	First Round

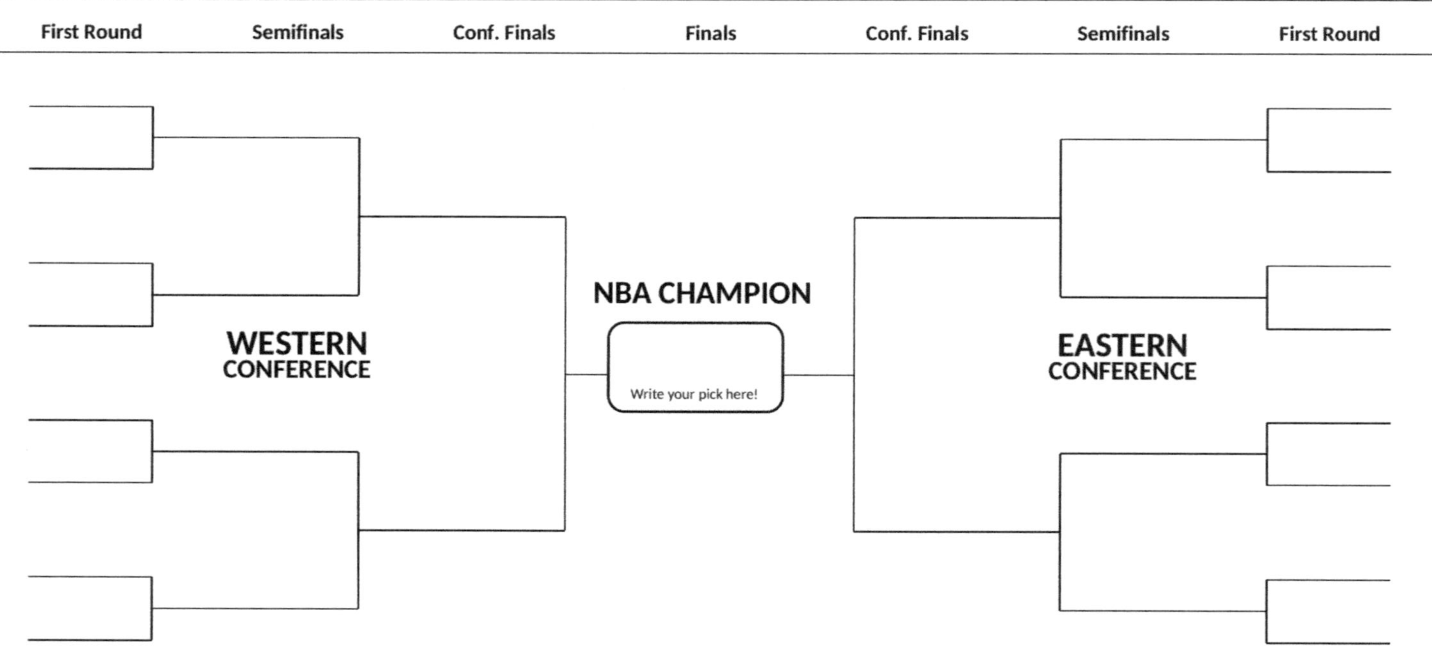

* Fill in your picks and try not to argue with your friends about it!

Part of the Fun Fan Facts: The Unofficial Sports Guide Series

Be the Boss of the Playoffs

You've broken down the matchups. You know which superstar takes over in the fourth quarter. You've seen the bench units that quietly decide series. You've watched the adjustments coaches make when their backs are against the wall.

Now it's time to stop watching and start deciding.

On this page, you are not just a fan. You are the Head Coach drawing up the last play with three seconds left on the clock. You are the GM who built this roster. You are the analyst who saw it all coming.

This is not just filling out a bracket.

This is building your championship run.

Sixteen teams enter the NBA Playoffs. The path is brutal. Best of seven. No shortcuts. No hiding. Every round gets louder, harder, and more personal.

This bracket is your Playoff Control Room.

The Game Plan

1. Survive Round One: Start with the opening round. Which matchup is going seven games? Who has the closer? Who folds under pressure? Make the calls.

2. Feel the Momentum: As you move into the Conference Semifinals and Conference Finals, things change. Role players become heroes. Stars feel the weight. Trust your reads.

3. Own the Finals: Trace your picks all the way to the NBA Finals. When the confetti falls and the trophy is raised, you'll find out who earned it.

House Rules: Circle your boldest upset. That is your official "I knew it" moment.

Choose Your Weapon: Pencil if you want flexibility. Pen if you trust your instincts. Sharpie if you believe in chaos.

Because once the playoffs tip off, there is no rewinding Game 7.

Make your picks. Trust your basketball brain. And let the playoff drama begin.

Fun Facts Wrap-Up

You made it through! You're officially a true superfan! Now it's time to put your knowledge to the test. Share these facts with friends and see who really knows their team best.

Love the series?

Your reviews help other fans discover Fun Fan Facts. If you enjoyed this book, we'd really appreciate you sharing your thoughts and leaving a review.

Want more Fun Fan Facts?

Scan the QR code below to visit our site and explore bonus trivia, challenges, and special extras - including new teams, future series, and collectible fun as they're released.

Collect All the Fun Fan Facts Series!

Check off every book you read. See the full set on Amazon. Search "Fun Fan Facts Jake Liam."

World Cup 2026 Edition

☐ Algeria	☐ France	☐ Paraguay
☐ Argentina	☐ Germany	☐ Portugal
☐ Australia	☐ Ghana	☐ Qatar
☐ Austria	☐ Haiti	☐ Saudi Arabia
☐ Belgium	☐ Iran	☐ Scotland
☐ Brazil	☐ Ivory Coast	☐ Senegal
☐ Canada	☐ Japan	☐ South Africa
☐ Cape Verde	☐ Jordan	☐ South Korea
☐ Colombia	☐ Mexico	☐ Spain
☐ Croatia	☐ Morocco	☐ Switzerland
☐ Curaçao	☐ Netherlands	☐ Tunisia
☐ Ecuador	☐ New Zealand	☐ United States
☐ Egypt	☐ Norway	☐ Uruguay
☐ England	☐ Panama	☐ Uzbekistan

World Cup 2026 Group Edition

☐ Group A	☐ Group E	☐ Group I
☐ Group B	☐ Group F	☐ Group J
☐ Group C	☐ Group G	☐ Group K
☐ Group D	☐ Group H	☐ Group L

English Football Edition

☐ Arsenal F.C.

☐ Aston Villa F.C.

☐ Chelsea F.C.

☐ Everton F.C.

☐ Fulham F.C.

☐ Liverpool F.C.

☐ Manchester City

☐ Manchester United

☐ Newcastle United F.C.

☐ Tottenham Hotspur

☐ West Ham United

☐ Wrexham A.F.C.

NBA Edition

☐ Atlanta Hawks

☐ Boston Celtics

☐ Brooklyn Nets

☐ Charlotte Hornets

☐ Chicago Bulls

☐ Cleveland Cavaliers

☐ Dallas Mavericks

☐ Denver Nuggets

☐ Detroit Pistons

☐ Golden State Warriors

☐ Houston Rockets

☐ Indiana Pacers

☐ LA Clippers

☐ Los Angeles Lakers

☐ Memphis Grizzlies

☐ Miami Heat

☐ Milwaukee Bucks

☐ Minnesota Timberwolves

☐ New Orleans Pelicans

☐ New York Knicks

☐ Oklahoma City Thunder

☐ Orlando Magic

☐ Philadelphia 76ers

☐ Phoenix Suns

☐ Portland Trail Blazers

☐ Sacramento Kings

☐ San Antonio Spurs

☐ Toronto Raptors

☐ Utah Jazz

☐ Washington Wizards

About the Author

Jake is a 13-year-old sports fan who loves football, American football, and basketball. He plays soccer as a goalie and dreams of one day playing for West Ham United and helping teach kids to love the game. His passion for sports runs in the family - his dad was a professional baseball player, and his stepdad sparked his love for West Ham. Through the Fun Fan Facts series, he shares the fun and excitement of sports with fans everywhere.